The CREEK INDIANS

The CREEK INDIANS

by **Grant Lyons**

Illustrated by David Kingham

JULIAN MESSNER NEW YORK

Manufactured in the United States of America

Design by David Kingham

Second Printing, 1979

Lyons, Grant.
    The Creek Indians.

    Includes index.
    SUMMARY: Discusses the history of the Creek
Indians and their powerful confederacy.
    1. Creek Indians—Juvenile literature.
[1. Creek Indians. 2. Indians of North America]
I. Kingham, David. II. Title.
E99.C9L95   970′.004′97   77-29255
ISBN 0-671-32985-6

FOR MY FATHER

MESSNER BOOKS BY GRANT LYONS

The Creek Indians

Andy Jackson and the Battles for New Orleans

Tales the People Tell in Mexico

CONTENTS

Chapter 1

IN THE BEGINNING

Even today the old people tell tales of the earliest days. They say that in the beginning the Muskogee people, or as we now call them, the Creeks, were born out of the earth itself. They crawled up out of the ground through a hole, like ants. They lived then in a far western land beside mountains that reached the sky. They called the mountains the backbone of the earth.

Then a thick fog descended upon the earth, sent by the Great Spirit, the Master of Breath. The Muskogee people could not see. They wandered around blindly, calling out to one another in fear. They drifted apart and became lost. The whole people were separated into small groups, and these groups stayed close to one another in fear of being entirely alone.

Finally, the Master of Breath had mercy. From the eastern edge of the world, where the sun rises, he began to blow at the fog. He blew and blew until the fog was gone. The people were joyful and sang a hymn of thanksgiving to the Master of Breath. And in each of the groups the people turned to each other and swore eternal brotherhood. They said that from then on the groups would be like large families—they would be as close to each other as brother and sister and father and son.

The group that was farthest to the east was the first to see the sun. They praised the wind that had blown the fog away and called themselves the Wind Family, or Clan. As the fog moved away from the other groups they, too, gave themselves names. Each group chose the name of the first animal it saw. So they became the Bear, Deer, Alligator, Raccoon, and Bird Clans. But the Wind Clan remained the most important clan of all.

The Muskogee found that they could not live in the western land. So they climbed a high mountain where they could see far to the west and far to the east. They decided to move to the east, where the sun rose. And so began a great march.

They traveled for a very long time, until they came to a river. The river was larger than any they had ever seen. It was black, and thick with mud. They crossed this river and went on. Then they came to another river, and this one flowed with water as red as blood. They crossed this river and stayed by its side awhile. But the sun still rose farther east, so they soon moved on again.

At last they came to a water too wide to cross—the ocean. So they turned back, and settled inland, by the rivers. They soon came to love this land. The soil was rich and gave them an abundance of corn, squash and pumpkins. The rivers were cool and good to drink.

The woods were full of animals to hunt. And the air
was warm almost all year long.

The land was good to the Muskogee. They
watched the autumn leaves dance in the wind, the
green buds in the spring, the ripening corn of summer,
with joy and gratitude toward the Master of Breath.

They had enemies, and were often at war, but they

managed to grow as a people until most of the other Indian peoples were afraid of them. And so the generations passed.

Later a pale-skinned people appeared in great canoes that seemed to fly over the water. They came from the east, across the wide water, from the rising sun. Seeing how the Muskogee built their villages on the rivers and creeks of their country, the Pale people called them "Creeks." So they have been called ever since.

Chapter 2

THE MUSKOGEE WAY

The Muskogee lived in what are now the states of Georgia and Alabama. Their towns and villages were built mainly on the Coosa, Tallapoosa, Flint, and Chattahoochee rivers. When the first Europeans began exploring North America, the Muskogee were among the most powerful and important Indians north of the Aztec empire of Mexico.

One reason the Muskogee were so powerful was the unusual government they had created. Unlike all their neighbors, they were not a single tribe. They were a league, or confederacy, of tribes living in different villages or towns over a wide area. Each town had its own chief, called a *mico*. But from time to time, and especially when war threatened, the micos of the various towns would meet together in a general council. At these great councils, war chiefs were elected and laws were passed that all Creeks were required to follow.

In many ways, the government of the Muskogee resembled the government of the United States when it was created many years later. The states—like the Muskogee towns—were largely independent, and the power of the central government—like that of the Muskogee councils—was limited.

The Muskogee system of government gave them a great advantage: their confederacy kept growing. Each time they won a war, the Muskogee offered the defeated tribe a chance to join their confederacy. Many accepted. By the time the first Europeans were building colonies in North America, there were approximately 10,000 members of what the whites called the Creek Confederacy.

In general, the Creeks held together, although sometimes one village would be at war while others were not. Fighting among the members of the confederation was strictly forbidden.

The system worked well because of the clans. Members of the same clans considered other members of their clans—even if they lived in a faraway village—as members of the same family. A member of the Wind Clan felt more loyalty to a member of his clan in another village than to the other clans in his own village. Thus the Creeks were both independent—and united.

The Creeks also divided their towns and their clans into the "red" and the "white." Red was the color of war. The war chief for the confederacy always came from a red clan. And peace talks were always held in a white town, led by a chief from a white clan. In a white town, in which the buildings were stained white, no man could be killed. But in times of war, the men of white town and red town, white clan and red clan, fought together against the common enemy.

War was very important to the Creeks. It was in

war that a young man could make his name known. By proving his skill and courage in battle, he earned the admiration of his people. No one could become rich among the Creeks. But a great warrior might be famous throughout the confederacy. Such a man could select the most beautiful women for his wives. He was respected and often received gifts from others.

Like other Indians of North America, the Creeks fought fiercely. They often tortured captured enemies. And they cut off the scalps of those they killed in battle. The scalps were then hung from the pole that stood at the center of every Creek town to show how successful that town had been in battle. But the Creeks were also generous to their enemies. Not only did they offer them a place in their confederacy, they often offered land to resettle those Indians driven from their own lands. When the early European settlers began to drive Indians away from the coast, the Creek confederacy grew faster than ever.

The Creek men were feared warriors and skilled hunters. They were excellent farmers. But they hunted and farmed only enough to live. And they lived mostly on their crops: corn, squash, pumpkins, beans, and sweet potatoes. The land they dug up, and planted, and harvested, did not belong to individual families. The entire town, both men and women, farmed the land together. Because of this no one could ever go hungry, unless the whole town did.

Apart from farming, the men and women had different jobs. While the men hunted, built buildings, made war, and governed, the women raised the children, cooked, and made the clothing. Women did not attend town councils or confederacy councils, but a wise woman was much respected and her advice was frequently sought.

The Creeks loved all sorts of sports. The favorite of the men was a wild ball game, so rough that injuries were common, and even deaths were not rare. The game was always played between a white town and a red town, and was called "brother to war." The Creeks recognized that the game was a substitute for real fighting, and so helped keep peace between towns.

Each of the players carried a thick stick with a small leather net, or basket, at one end. The ball was made of deerskin-covered hair, and was about the size of a golf ball. Using the sticks, the players carried and tossed the ball the length of a special field set aside for the game and threw it between two poles, like goalposts. What made the game so rough was that the players were free to do anything to get the ball from an opponent, from wrestling to beating him with the stick!

Another, quieter, form of the stickball game was played between men and women. Other games included bowling and chunkey. The chunkey yard was a square at the center of each village. A stone disc, hollowed out at the center and beautifully polished, was rolled across the square and contestants tried to hit it with their spears as it rolled along.

From birth, Creek boys were treated differently from Creek girls. The boys were wrapped in cougar furs, to take on that animal's fierceness. The girls wore deer or bison skins. Punishments were rare. Boys especially were not supposed to be punished by their mothers. If a little boy had to be punished, he was usually scratched with sharp spines by an uncle, one of his mother's brothers. The marks from the scratching showed for days, and so the boy would be teased by the other children.

The boys played the same games as the men. When they played "brother to war," of course, they were not so rough. But their favorite sport was foot racing. A warrior, or a good ball player, had to be able to run very far and very fast and this was good training.

Chunkey—a fiercely played sport

The boys also had contests. They might allow themselves to be stung by yellow jackets (a type of wasp), for instance, to see which of them could bear the most stings. And much of their day was spent wandering together through the woods, practicing with their bows and arrows on small animals and targets.

The girls were not given the same freedom as the boys. They stayed with the women and helped them with their work, tending the gardens, keeping the fires going, making pottery and baskets.

Before the white men came, Creek clothing was very simple. As long as the weather was not very cold,

the men wore almost nothing at all—a square skin hung from a strip of rawhide around the waist, and perhaps a grass blanket draped over one shoulder. Women also wore a skin hung from the waist, but theirs was longer, and they wore a kind of grass shawl over their right shoulders. Children usually wore nothing at all in warm weather. When a boy or girl reached 12 or 13 it was time to dress as an adult. Moccasins were worn when the weather was cold, or by the men when they were traveling for long distances to hunt or make war. Otherwise the Creeks went barefoot.

The Creeks believed that the world is full of invisible spirits. The greatest spirit was the Master of Breath, who gave the breath of life or took it away. Lesser spirits inhabited certain trees, ponds, and streams. Some of these spirits were good, some dangerous. A particularly dangerous spirit was the "tie-snake." This spirit lived in a particular part of a particular stream. When someone went near that part of the water, the tie-snake might wrap itself around its victim and take him or her away to the underworld forever.

Water and fire were sacred to the Creeks and most of their ceremonies centered on one or the other. The first duty of every Creek every morning was to bathe in the nearby river or stream, even in very cold weather. And in each village the sacred council fire had to be kept burning night and day. This fire was extinguished only at the time of the Green Corn Dance.

The Green Corn Dance was the most important event in the Creek year. It took place in late summer, when the new corn had all been harvested. The men drank a special tea, made from a root. The tea was called "the black drink." It made them vomit, and was meant to purify their bodies. The black drink also gave the men energy for dancing the Corn Dance all night. On the last day of the ceremonies, the council fire was put out. A new fire was started, always with seven different kinds of wood. This meant a new year had begun, and all old grudges must be forgiven and forgotten.

The Creeks felt their life was happy and free. They did not have to work very hard, yet they were comfortable. Freedom was extremely important. The town councils and the councils of the Creek confederacy did not interfere very much in the daily life of the individual Creeks. There were few crimes. The man or woman who did violate the law was usually punished by clan or family, not by the tribe or town. Punishments were harsh—a nose cut off, whipping, or death.

The Creeks loved their mother, the earth, and they lived close to her. They sang songs of praise to the trees, rivers, and the animals of the woods and meadows. In the summer they lived in roofless houses so they could see the stars and feel the breezes and hear the streams running and splashing day and night. Only when the weather became cold did they move inside their stick-and-mud huts.

And then one day something happened . . .

Chapter 3

THE CREEKS DISCOVER
THE WHITE MAN

In the early spring of the year 1540, the small Creek village of Toa (in what is now southern Georgia) was quietly going about its business. The weather was mild and the dogwood was blooming. Suddenly, out of the surrounding woods, wild monsters appeared, waving long knives and spitting fire from sticks. These monsters had four legs and two heads. One of the heads was like a human's, but pale, with dark hair all over it. The other head was shiny, and glittered in the sun. The people of Toa fled into the woods in terror.

But not all escaped. And when those who had been captured looked closer, they saw that these monsters were really pale-skinned men with hair on their faces, wearing headpieces they called helmets. They rode on the backs of large animals they called horses. These strange men had a chief. He forced the captured men and women of Toa to come with him and his men, to carry their belongings and act as their servants.

The chief's name was Hernando DeSoto. He and his men were Spanish explorers. They had marched up from Florida, looking for gold. DeSoto was determined to find gold. He didn't care how far into the wilderness he had to go to find it. Nor did he care what he had to do to get it.

The next village on DeSoto's path was Ichisi, on

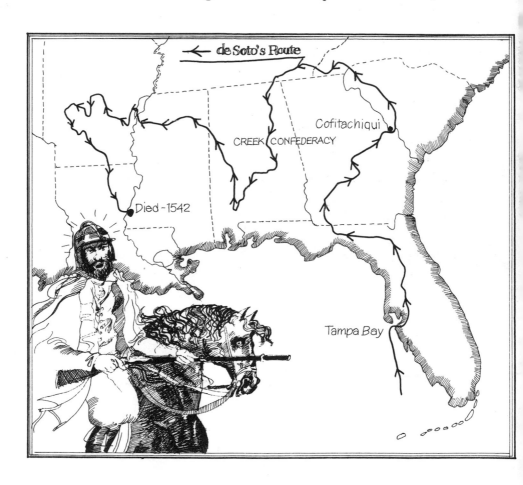

the Flint River, in Georgia. But the people of Ichisi got word of the approach of the monsters and fled before they arrived. DeSoto's men ran some of them down in the woods and demanded that the mico be brought to him.

Although it was difficult to tell what it was the pale-skinned people wanted, the mico of Ichisi figured it out at last. They wanted gold, and a beautiful princess. He told DeSoto that the village of Ichisi had neither. Farther to the northeast, however, lay the land of the Princess of Cofitachiqui. She was beautiful, and might have gold. DeSoto thanked the mico. He and his men, unable to find anything better, ate all the dogs in the village. Then they took their captives and made them carry their belongings toward the northeast.

The Princess of Cofitachiqui ruled the Catawba Indians north of the Savannah River (the present western North Carolina and South Carolina). At the time, the Catawbas were at war with some of the Creek villages, including Ichisi. So the clever mico had sent the Spanish dog-eaters to prey upon his enemies!

On their way to Cofitachiqui, the Spaniards approached a large Creek town called Altamaca (near the present city of Macon, Georgia). But they could not cross the Ocmulgee River, swollen with the spring floods, to reach the village. The mico of Altamaca sent a welcome to DeSoto and offered to bring him and his men over in canoes. DeSoto accepted, and upon his arrival in the village presented the mico with a splendid white feather. The mico, pleased by the gift, promised to eat and sleep with the feather for the rest of his life. He also offered to help the Spaniards on their way to the Princess of Cofitachiqui.

And so DeSoto moved on, chasing his dream of

gold and a beautiful princess. In each village he passed through, he erected a cross. His men kneeled before the cross and prayed. DeSoto explained briefly to the Indians the doctrines of Christianity, and then men and women were rounded up to serve as slaves on the long march.

DeSoto crossed the Savannah River, and passed out of Creek country into the land of the Catawbas. He found the Princess of Cofitachiqui, but she was neither young nor beautiful and she had no gold.

The Princess told DeSoto he might find gold in the mountains to the west, and DeSoto turned in that direction. He wandered for months in the southern Appalachian mountains, looking for gold, but finding nothing. In the mountains there were fewer Indian villages to loot, and there was no sign of any gold. So his men grew resentful and restless.

Finally, the Spaniards turned back south and once again entered the country of the Creeks. DeSoto had heard of a wealthy Creek town called Coosa. It was midsummer now. His men suffered from the heat and insects, and they were desperately hungry.

The people of Coosa had heard about the Spaniards, too. They were afraid, but curious. The mico of the town had himself carried to DeSoto on the shoulders of his strongest warriors. He wore a cloak of rich furs, a brilliant crown of feathers, and sat on a cushion as he was carried along. Around him, men and women played flutes and danced.

The mico welcomed the white men and said to DeSoto:

"Superior lord, although I come but now to meet you, it is a long time since I received you in my heart."

DeSoto promptly took the chief prisoner, along

with all the other leading men of the village. Then his men fell upon the new corn, which was just being harvested. Twenty-five days later, when there was nothing more to eat, they put the mico, his sister, and many others in chains and continued their march south.

Taking the mico of Coosa prisoner helped the Spaniards more than they foresaw. Coosa was the leading village of all the Creeks. No Creek village dared to oppose the Spaniards for fear that harm might come to the mico of Coosa. DeSoto and his men moved easily through the Creek country, eating the Indians' corn and taking slaves.

When, at last, the white men left Creek country, DeSoto released the mico of Coosa. But he held the mico's sister and she was never seen again.

The village of Coosa was destroyed. The people fled to the woods to eat nuts and wild game. And all through the Creek country, people starved that winter. Now that the white men were in North America, nothing would ever be the same.

In fact, the whole world was in for many changes. The discovery of America would change Europe almost as much as it changed America. The leading nations of Europe all saw the New World as a giant treasure chest, full of gold, silver, and what was more precious than either—*land*. The race among nations to see who could get the most from this treasure chest began.

In time, the battle for the riches of the New World narrowed down to three nations: Spain, Great Britain, and France. It so happened that in North America the lands of the Creeks lay right between the claims of all three.

The Spanish claims were to the south. They

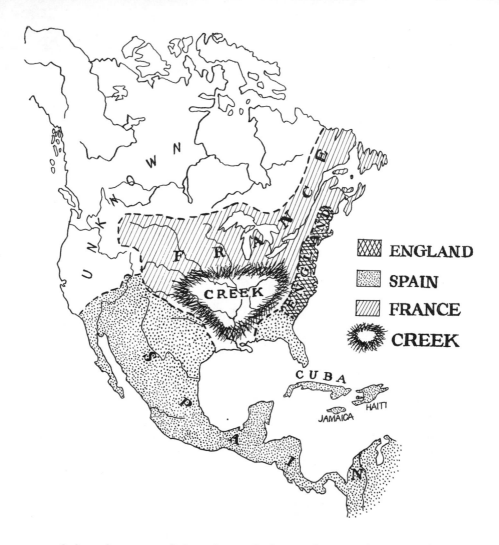

ENGLAND

SPAIN

FRANCE

CREEK

claimed most of South and Central America, Mexico, and Florida. The Florida Indians were forced to work on Spanish plantations, and in exchange they were taught Christianity. To the north of Florida lay the lands of the Creeks.

The French claimed eastern Canada and the Mississippi River valley, which they called Louisiana. They built a town near the mouth of the Mississippi, called

New Orleans. Further east, another French settlement, Mobile, was established on Mobile Bay. The lands of the Creeks lay east of these French towns.

The British claimed much of the Atlantic coast of North America. Much more than the other two nations, Great Britain sent its men and women to live in the new lands. The English settlers established farms and towns, and called themselves colonies. These colonies stretched from Massachusetts to Charleston, on the coast, just north of the Savannah River, in what was then called Carolina. To the south and west lay the lands of the Creeks.

The Creeks sometimes visited the English colony of Charleston to trade. They brought furs and deerskins and traded them for guns, pots, pans, needles, axes, and other metal tools, and for the bright

colored cloth the English made so well. Less often, the Creeks also traded with the Spanish in Florida. They had no friendly contact for some time with the French, who had made friends of the Choctaws—traditional enemies of the Creeks.

The English, French, and Spanish had large wars and small wars among themselves, as each nation struggled to get more of the New World for itself. Through most of these, the Creeks remained neutral, taking no sides. But in 1702, the English at last convinced them to help in a war against Spain and France. A group of Creeks and Englishmen went into Florida and destroyed many of the Spanish plantations. To the west, the Creeks defeated the French and Choctaws and came close to capturing Mobile.

The English won the war, and the Creeks became more powerful than ever. They were beginning to play a role in world history.

Chapter 4

THE AMBASSADORS

It was the year 1734, and everyone in the great city of London was excited. Ambassadors of a nation thousands of miles across the sea had just arrived to sign a treaty with Great Britain. But these representatives were unlike any that had ever been seen in London before. They walked about almost naked! They wore feathers in their long hair! They were the ambassadors of the Creek nation.

The chief ambassador was named Tomochichi. He was an old man, but he had sailed across the great Atlantic Ocean on the flying canoe of the English in order to meet with King George II. Tomochichi had come at the request of a friend, James Oglethorpe, an Englishman whom the Creeks liked and respected. The purpose of the meeting was to sign a treaty granting Oglethorpe the right to begin a new English colony on Creek lands. This new colony would be called Georgia, after the English king.

The land the Creeks were giving up lay in what is now southeastern Georgia, along the coast south of the Savannah River, and it extended up the river about a hundred miles. There the town of Augusta had been founded. The Creeks did not look on this land as important to them. They were willing to give it up in return for certain things they wanted from the British. And this is what Tomochichi wanted to tell the British king.

Tomochichi

Oglethorpe had several reasons for wanting to begin a new colony here. For one thing, he wanted to make certain that the Spanish did not take this land. The Spanish claimed that their colony of Florida extended all the way north to the Savannah River. The English disagreed.

Also, Oglethorpe wanted to settle Georgia with English people who faced prison terms in Britain for

James Oglethorpe

unpaid debts. Rather than go to prison or starve, these people could begin a new life in the American wilderness. Thus, both Great Britain and its people would be well served.

Oglethorpe also wanted to strengthen friendly relations with the Creek confederacy. The English recognized that the Creeks held the key to the control of much of North America. Creeks and Englishmen had fought together. But the Creeks were shrewd. They did not cut off relations with Britain's enemies, Spain and France. In fact, they were friendlier with both these nations than ever before. They did not want the English to take their friendship for granted.

Now Tomochichi and the other Creek ambassadors had come to London to negotiate. They were carried to the court of King George in a golden carriage, wearing their usual skins, but covered by fur cloaks dyed crimson and gold. In their hair they wore many feathers. The people of London lined the streets and crowded around the palace to catch a glimpse of the Indians. And the Indians, too, looked at the great smoky city, with its thousands and thousands of people, with amazement and curiosity.

When Tomochichi was asked what he thought of London, he surprised many with his answer. He had noticed the smoke that hung over the city, and the way the people were all crowded together, living on top of one another. Tomochichi said he was surprised that the English were so foolish—they built houses so strong they lasted longer than the people who lived in them! What was the point of that? The palace and public buildings were very beautiful, indeed, but he did not think the people of London were as happy as the Creeks.

Tomochichi gave King George a great bundle of white eagle feathers as a token of peace and friendship. Then he told the king what his people wanted in exchange for the land they were giving up. They wanted more and better English goods, brought to them through the new colony of Georgia. They wanted definite and unchanging weights and measures for the furs and skins they traded for these goods. And they wanted the king to keep Christian missionaries and rum out of all Creek lands. To all this the king and his advisors readily agreed.

When the agreement was concluded, and all the ceremonies finished, the Creeks sailed home. There they reported all they had seen and done. Soon the word spread to all the Creek villages: the English were wealthy and powerful, but they were fair.

The Georgia colony did draw the Creeks closer to Britain. And the Creek way of life slowly changed. They learned European methods of farming, and replaced the digging stick with the plow. They bought metal tools and cooking utensils and soon forgot how to make their own from clay and wood. They learned to use guns instead of bows and arrows.

The English goods made life easier for the Creeks. But they also made problems. Some of the better hunters, with more skins and furs to trade, grew wealthier than others. These others began to run up bills with the traders that were too high for them to pay.

In spite of their ties with the English, most Creeks tried to remain friends of the Spanish and French as well. They allowed the French to build a fort, Fort Toulouse, on Creek land in what is now Alabama. The French and Spanish tried to get the Creeks to join their wars against Great Britain. But the Creeks remained

Creek chief "Deer-Without-a-Heart" and his daughter Chee-a-ex-e-co.
Their clothing is much different from the simple clothes shown
on page 19, and shows how Europeans influenced Indian dress.

neutral, and did not take sides. After a while, the Creeks began to argue among themselves as to which nation they should favor

In 1756, the French and Indian War began. The French and English fought each other in Europe, America and Asia. The French tried to get all the Indians who lived near English colonies to attack them. Some of these Indians had already been pushed off their land by the English settlers. They believed that the English settlements had to be destroyed or there would be no room left for the Indians anywhere. And so many Indians joined the attack against the English colonies.

But the Creeks refused to help the French. And the English won, forcing the French to give up all their colonies in Canada. By secret treaty, France gave all of Louisiana to Spain, to keep the English from getting that, too. Now only Spain and Britain remained in the fight for control of North America. And of the two, Great Britain was clearly the stronger.

The Creeks had made the right decision in refusing to fight against their English friends. And for a few years, the British seemed to have everything their own way in America. But then new and unexpected difficulties arose. Britain's own colonies rose up in revolt, demanding independence. War broke out—this time a war between English people. The Creeks didn't know what to do. Which side was friend and which side was enemy in *this* war?

Chapter 5

THE AMERICANS

The Creeks were not aware of the issues that led the American colonists to break away from Great Britain. But if they had read the Declaration of Independence, they would have seen that it was not written for them. The Declaration of Independence referred to the Indians as "merciless Indian savages," and blamed the king for giving them guns.

The Creeks tried to get the English and Americans to make peace. One Creek mico sent a peace offering to the British Indian agent—an eagle wing and tobacco for the peace pipe. He told the agent: "We thought that all the English people were one people. But now we hear that they have differences among themselves. It is our desire that they drop their disputes and not spoil one another."

Several of the traders that the Creeks liked were American rebels. They urged the Creeks to fight the British. But other men the Creeks admired remained loyal to the British. They told the Creeks to remain neutral and fight no one.

The Americans drove the English out of Savannah and Augusta in the Georgia colony. Now the English had to send traders and goods up from Pensacola, in Spanish Florida, to trade with the Creeks. But most of the guns and other equipment the English sent were captured by the Americans.

The Cherokees, who lived north of the Creeks, joined the British side. They had seen much of their land stolen by American settlers. They hoped that if the British won, the settlers would be forced to stay off Cherokee land. But the American settlers formed an army and attacked the main Cherokee villages, killing many. The Creeks were warned that the same thing could happen to them.

The Creeks were divided among themselves. Many wanted to join the British, for Georgia settlers were beginning to move onto Creek land, too. Others said that the best policy was to join neither side. Still others said that the Americans were their neighbors and friends, and they had best help them. The disagreement became so hot that the Creeks almost had a war among themselves. In the meantime, no supplies reached the Creek villages. In the winter of 1777-78, they all suffered.

Although Great Britain was the most powerful nation in the world, she could not seem to defeat the determined American rebels. A large British army tried to invade the rebellious colonies from Canada, which had refused to take part in the revolt. But that army was defeated by a smaller American army at Saratoga, New York. This defeat of the British convinced Spain and France that the Americans really

Which side in the War of Independence should the Creeks support —British or American?

might win their independence. So Spain sent money and France sent a fleet to help the Americans. The French ships drove the British out of Pensacola and Mobile. But, in the meantime, the British had recaptured Savannah, and much of the Georgia colony.

The most important and influential Creek leader at this time was Alexander McGillivray. He was the son of a Scottish trader and a Creek-French woman of the Wind clan, and had received a white man's education. He tried very hard to convince the Creeks to fight the Americans. McGillivray recognized that the greatest enemy of the Creeks was the American settler, always looking for more land. Eventually McGillivray had his way. Creek raiding parties began attacking Georgia settlements. But not all the Creeks turned against the Americans.

In December of 1780, the anti-American Creeks fought their most important battle in the War for American Independence. The English had just captured Augusta, and invited the Creeks to join them there for talks and supplies. But even as the Creeks arrived, the Americans counterattacked.

And the battle was not fought Indian-style, in the woods, with trees for cover. It was fought out in the open field near the town. But the Creeks formed themselves in rows, like English soldiers, and held their ground. Many men were killed on both sides, but the Americans were eventually driven back. Georgians would not soon forget this stinging defeat at the hands of the Creeks.

The war dragged on, but the willingness of the English to keep up the struggle faded. Even before the English gave up, the Creeks decided to open peace talks with the Americans. But the Americans were hard bargainers. They would make peace with the Creeks only if the Creeks agreed to give a large strip of their land to the new state of Georgia. Reluctantly, the Creeks agreed. Georgia settlers had already begun moving onto much of the land anyway. At least, the Indians hoped, the agreement would stop the settlers where they were.

The peace treaty that ended the war did not mention the Creek nation. It said that all the land between Canada and Spanish Florida, from the Atlantic to the Mississippi, belonged to the new nation, the United States of America. The state of Georgia shortly claimed the land to their west as far as the Mississippi, just as though the Creeks were not there.

To the Creeks, the land they lived on and hunted belonged to them all, as a people. It had been given to them by the Master of Breath. None of this land belonged to any *one* Indian. The only way any of the land could be given up or sold was by the agreement of the whole Creek Council. From their point of view, there was no separation between their people and their land. One Creek mico told an Indian Commissioner from the new United States:

"Our lands are our life and breath. If we part with them we part with our blood."

But the Americans did not look at it this way. To them, the Creeks now lived on land belonging to the United States. Officials of the state of Georgia invited a few Creek micos in, gave them a few presents, and got them to sign a paper they didn't completely understand. The paper said that certain Creek lands were being sold to Georgia for further white settlement. Immediately, settlers began moving onto these lands.

The Creeks called a meeting of their great council. Overwhelmingly, this council voted to reject the treaty giving away this land. But the state of Georgia paid no attention. When Creeks did not move off this disputed land, they were shot at.

Alexander McGillivray was still the leading man among the Creeks. His white father had returned to Britain when the Americans won the war, but McGillivray stayed on among the Creeks. He believed his people were still an independent nation. So he went to Pensacola to speak to the Spanish. The Spanish were very friendly. They were afraid the United States was planning to try to take away Florida, or Louisiana. The Creeks would be useful friends. The Spanish agreed to trade with the Creeks from Pensacola and to protect them against the Americans, if necessary.

Spain was not really stroι.g enough to protect the Creeks any better than they could protect themselves. Nevertheless, leaders of the United States became alarmed. They invited McGillivray and other prominent Creeks to New York, then the capital of the new nation, for talks.

Just as Tomochichi had gone to London to meet with King George, McGillivray and 26 other leading Creeks now went to New York to meet with the new Secretary of War, Henry Knox. By wagon and horseback, they traveled northward through Georgia, the

Henry Knox

Carolinas, Virginia, Maryland, and Pennsylvania. Everywhere the Americans turned out to watch the proud Creeks pass by on their way to the historic meeting. At New York, the Indians were received in a solemn public ceremony by the new United States Congress.

After lengthy discussion, McGillivray agreed to sign the treaty offered by the United States. The Creeks gave up only part of the land under dispute. More important than this, however, the Creeks recognized the authority of the United States. In return, they were promised that the lands remaining to them would be protected from further invasion by white settlers.

With this treaty, called the Treaty of New York, the Creeks believed that they had firmly established a lasting peace with the United States. But the promise that their lands would be protected from further white settlement was worthless. The Georgians ignored the federal government's treaty. They settled on land the treaty had promised to the Creeks. And they moved even further. The settlers went deep into Creek hunting grounds with dogs, killing all the game. Their cattle ranged freely onto Creek farmlands, damaging their crops. The Creeks were bitter at the broken promises of the United States.

Chapter 6

RED STICK OR WHITE?

Benjamin Hawkins rode his horse into the Creek town of Tuckabachee on a pleasant fall morning in the fall of 1812. He was the agent for the United States to the Creeks, and he had called a meeting of the leading micos. The village was crowded. Hawkins hadn't expected so many to come to hear him.

He wondered if they had heard the news already: the United States and Great Britain were again at war. If they had, no doubt they had heard it from one of those infernal British agents. The British had been trying to stir up trouble among the Creeks for years. That was the reason he had called this meeting.

The meeting, Hawkins felt, was extremely important. Great Britain was the most powerful nation in the world. So powerful, in fact, that the British seemed to think they could make the United States into one of their colonies again. And so it was war again. But if they were to survive this war, the powerful Creeks must be convinced to stay out of it.

The next day Hawkins sat in a crowded council house with all the important chiefs. He was nervous. Something was up, he was sure of that. But what? Whenever he asked one of his Creek friends, the man would turn away without answering.

Hawkins explained to the Creek chiefs why the United States had declared war on Great Britain. But they hardly seemed to be listening to him. They all seemed to be *waiting*. For what? It was as though they were in a hurry for him to finish.

Hawkins knew he had a difficult job. He tried to convince the micos that the United States was their friend. But then one of the Creeks asked him: When

Benjamin Hawkins tried to reassure the Indians of the "White Man's" good intentions

would the United States begin to keep its promises? The Creeks had given up land. They had refused to take up the Red Stick of war. Again and again they had been promised the lands they held would be left alone by the white settlers. But again and again the promises had been broken. In fact, the Creek word for the Georgians meant "people-ever-greedy-for-land."

Hawkins did not really have an answer. Secretary Knox was sympathetic to the Creeks. But he believed there was no way to stop the flood of settlers. Instead, he tried to change the Indians' way of life. He sent Christian missionaries and teachers into the Creek country. He hoped that in time the Creeks would become just like the white settlers, each with a little farm, working for their families alone. They would simply disappear in the flood of white settlers.

Knox's policy had some success. Many Creeks *had* become wealthy in the years since the War of American Independence. Some owned plantations and slaves. And many of the leading Creeks were sons and daughters of white men who had married Creek women and lived among the Creeks. These mixed-bloods were often more sympathetic with white men's ways than with Indian ways. Hawkins was counting on the mixed-bloods to keep the Creeks peaceful during the war with Britain.

But as Hawkins was promising once again that the United States would protect the Creek lands, a startling thing happened. Dozens of strangely dressed Indians entered the council house. Everyone in the building fell silent.

Hawkins knew at a glance that these were not Creeks. They were dressed in the style of the Indians of the north, the Shawnees. They wore no white man's

46

clothing at all. Their almost naked bodies were brightly painted—for war. From the awed silence of those sitting in the council house, Hawkins recognized that the Shawnees, not he, were the reason the village was so crowded.

The man who led these Indians was none other than the great Shawnee chief, Tecumseh. Tecumseh was a Shawnee, but his mother had been a Creek, so he had close ties with the Creek confederacy. For years he

Tecumseh and his band of Shawnees listen in silence to the arguments in the Creek council house.

and his brother, called "the Prophet," had been trying to get all the Indians of the Ohio Valley to unite and fight the Americans. The Shawnees and some other tribes had already gone to war. Tecumseh and his Shawnees had been defeated by the Americans in the battle of Tippecanoe the year before. Now that Great Britain was at war with the United States, he was trying to get all the remaining Indians to rise up together against the Americans.

Tecumseh and his men marched in and sat silently near the front of the council house. They said nothing, and did not even look at the white man. And so Hawkins had to go on with his arguments, while every Indian about him sat silently.

Hawkins and the Creek chiefs met for several days. Every day Tecumseh and his warriors entered in their war paint and sat, silent and defiant, near the front. The Creeks made it clear to Hawkins that they wanted him to go away. Finally, since he was getting nowhere, Hawkins left Tuckabachee.

Now, with the white man gone, Tecumseh did speak. He always had a great gift for exciting Indians with his speeches. And this time was no exception. Tecumseh's message was that the ways of the white man were evil. The Indian must return to his ancient ways before it was too late. As long as he lived near the white man, the Indian became weaker and his gods became angrier.

Look at the Creeks, he said. Once a proud and mighty people, now the fools of the white men. They had come to desire the white man's goods so much they could not live without them. They ran up debts to the traders and had to pay these debts with their lands, with their very breath. And even so, the white settlers did not leave them in peace. And now the white man was telling them how to govern themselves, to forget the red and the white. The white man wanted to say who the Creek chiefs would be. The white man wanted to separate them from each other so he could take away their land.

The time had come, Tecumseh said, to snatch up the Red Stick of war. If the Indians joined together, with the help of the English, they could drive the Americans out of North America. If they did not do it now, the time would come when none of the Creek lands would be safe. Already the Americans were planning to force all the Indians to move west of the Mississippi River. For the Americans had bought more land from the French—the land they called the Louisiana Territory. The United States now reached to the great Rocky Mountains—the backbone of the earth! The white men were eating up the whole earth!

After speaking thus to the Creeks, Tecumseh returned north of the Ohio to the Shawnees. But he left the Creeks excited. Many wanted to take up the Red Stick. Others argued that Tecumseh was a great man, but he was only a tool of the English. The Americans were on the land, and would not go away even if they lost the war. The Creeks would have to learn to live with them. The British might promise many things today. But tomorrow they would be gone, back across the Mother of Waters. The Creeks would then have to face the Americans alone.

But those whom Tecumseh had convinced would not listen to these arguments. Angrily they returned to their own villages. They destroyed their plows, their hogs, their cattle, their cloth, their metal tools, for all these were the evil things of the white men. But they did not destroy their guns. Around their council fires they danced a new dance—"The Dance of the Lakes" Tecumseh had called it. This dance would bring back the favor of their gods. With this dance, they would drive the white men off their lands forever.

Chapter 7

THE RED STICK WAR

Tecumseh left the Creeks divided among themselves as they never had been before. But for a year or so the war between the United States and Great Britain seemed far away. The Creeks who wanted war, called the Red Sticks, or "Upper Creeks," were kept in check by their chiefs. But there were a few small fights, and these led eventually to war.

On one occasion, a number of Creeks returning from a trading trip to Pensacola were attacked by Georgians. There were dead on both sides. Then a group of Creek warriors, on their way back from a talk with Tecumseh, fell upon a white settlement and killed seven families. Immediately, the word spread—the Creeks were on the warpath!

The leading chiefs of the Creeks at that time were William McIntosh and Menewa. Both were part white. When they learned which Creeks had killed the white settlers, they had these men brought to them and killed. They sent word to the government of the United States, telling what they had done. They did not want war. But before anyone knew what was happening, the Creeks drifted into war against themselves—civil war. The relatives of the men killed by Menewa and William McIntosh's orders began taking revenge on the other Creeks who had been involved. And the relatives of *these* men, in turn, began to seek *their* revenge. Family turned against family, village against village. Menewa himself was threatened.

The government of the United States did not want war with the Creeks either. Although the Creeks were no longer unified, they were still by far the most powerful group of Indians on the frontier.

But the Whites on the frontier were another matter. They wanted to be rid of the Creeks. The Creeks occupied valuable land that white people wanted to settle on. Also, the Creeks were thought to be much too dangerous to have as neighbors. They wanted all the Indians cleared out and forced to move further west. War would give them an opportunity to drive the Indians off the frontier once and for all.

White men from Georgia and Tennessee began raiding Creek villages as early as 1811. The American government had its hands full with Great Britain. It could do nothing to stop these raids. The soldiers were often members of the states' citizen armies, called militia. The raids forced more and more Creeks to join the Red Stick party and to fight the settlers. The Red Stick people were also known as Upper Creeks, since most of them came from the northern and western section of the Creek country—Alabama.

In June of 1812, the Creeks began counterattacking. Settlers became frightened and moved into hastily built forts for protection. One of these, Fort Mims, was erected on the Alabama River, in the heart of the Upper Creek area. It was here that the fighting became a war—the Red Stick War, also known as the Creek War.

The fort had been badly built. In fact, it was hardly a fort at all—it was more of a stockade (log wall), built around the house of a farmer named Samuel Mims. The gate to the stockade was so crooked that it could be opened and closed only with difficulty, so it was usually left open. The men guarding the fort were not careful. They failed to post guards or patrols to keep a lookout for Indians. One day, two slaves returned from grazing cattle outside the fort and reported that they had seen some Indians, all painted for war. No one believed them, and they were beaten for lying. Though they saw Indians the next day, too, they did not dare say so.

The Indians were Red Stick Creeks, led by a half-white named William Weatherford but known as Red Eagle among his people. On August 30, 1813, Red Eagle ordered his men to attack Fort Mims. His warriors rushed down on the fort and, finding the gate open, poured in. The battle was short and bloody. Almost everyone in the fort—men, women and children—was killed, all in a few minutes. Red Eagle tried to stop the killing, but by then it was too late.

One of the Creeks recognized a woman in the fort who had once been kind to him. Instead of killing her and her children, he took them prisoner, saying he wanted them for slaves. Then he slipped away from the other Indians and kept the woman and children alive for weeks in the woods. He hunted game for her and hid her from other Indians until he could deliver her safely to a white settlement.

The "massacre of Fort Mims," as it was called, shocked the frontier settlers. Three armies of militia immediately entered Creek country, looking for vengeance. One of these, moving south from Tennessee, was led by "Jacksa Chula Harjo," "Jackson-old-and-fierce," or Andrew Jackson, later to become our seventh president.

Jackson understood very well that the Creeks were divided amongst themselves. His army included not only Tennessee militia, but also friendly Creeks, Cherokees and Choctaws. The Creeks that remained

Andrew Jackson

The Creeks called him "Jacksa Chula Harjo" (Jackson-Old-and-Fierce)

friendly to the Americans lived mostly in southern Georgia. They were known as the Lower Creeks. Without these Indians, Jackson would have had a very small army. They marched across Creek territory, burning villages to the ground.

The Red Sticks, including Menewa, fought Jackson in battle after battle. But they were always badly outnumbered, and defeated. Desperate, they moved to sacred ground to fight. But the sacred ground of the Creeks did not stop bullets or flames.

At Tallusahatchee, Jackson did what the Creeks had done at Fort Mims. The village was not defended. Still, Jackson's troops killed every man, woman and child in the village. One of the frontiersmen with Jackson, a young man named Davy Crockett, reported seeing the

Davy Crockett was not proud of his role in the massacre at Tallusahatchee.

body of a woman with 20 bullet holes in her. He added, "We shot them like dogs." He wasn't proud of the fact. Later, at the village of Artussee, 200 men, women and children were trapped and burned alive. At Talladega, Jackson defeated and killed more than 500 warriors.

But Jackson was not satisfied. He wanted to destroy the Red Sticks completely—and he wanted the man responsible for the raid on Fort Mims, Red Eagle.

At the Battle of Ecunchate, it looked as if Jackson had finally caught his man. The Red Sticks were defeated and Red Eagle himself was trapped. He fled to the banks of the Alabama River, racing ahead of Jackson's men. And at the river there was no place to go, for there was a steep cliff, with the river far below. Red Eagle did not want to be captured—he could guess how he would be treated by Jackson. So he dug his heels into the sides of his great gray horse. Horse and rider together went flying out into the air and down into the swift-flowing Alabama.

When Jackson's men arrived at the river, it was as though Red Eagle had disappeared into thin air. But then they saw him, moving swiftly away in the river's current. One hand held the mane of his gray horse, the other held his rifle high. He had escaped.

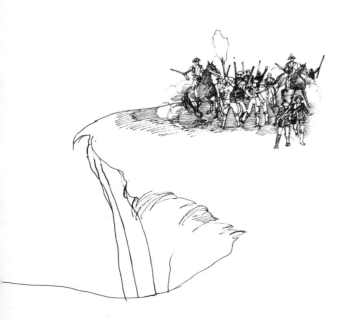

The Red Sticks' last stand was made near the Creek village of Tohopeka, in a horseshoe-shaped bend of the Tallapoosa River, in eastern Alabama. The river surrounded the Red Sticks on three sides. On the fourth side they built a barricade and took cover behind it. Menewa led the Red Stick Creeks. Bill McIntosh led the Creeks with Jackson. And among the Cherokees with Jackson was a giant white man who had been adopted by the tribe, and was one of Jackson's best friends—Sam Houston.

Nine hundred Red Sticks stood their ground and fought to the last man. When the bloody battle was over, only 70 were left alive.

One of those still alive was Menewa. He was shot seven times in the battle and left for dead. Then as the

Menewa, one of the few Red Sticks to survive, was hit seven times by rifle bullets - but escaped into the Tallapoosa River

SITE OF THE RED STICK WAR

white troops were moving among the dead, Menewa regained consciousness. A warrior to the end, he fired his rifle at the nearest soldier. Another soldier immediately ran up and shot him through the head. But still Menewa did not die. He awoke again after dark. He dragged his bullet-riddled body to the river bank and slipped into the water. Floating with the current, he came eventually to where the Red Sticks' women and children were hiding. They nursed him back to health. But his days as a warrior were over.

Jackson wrote to President James Madison that he believed he had broken the strength of the Creeks for all time. He was right. And he had his reward. Madison appointed him to head all the American armies of the South against the British. He would soon meet the British in a fight for the city of New Orleans. Winning that battle would make him a hero for all Americans. It would lead, in fourteen more years, to his election as president of the United States.

One night, as Jackson sat in camp, a young man slipped very quietly into his tent. He was an Indian, but he was unarmed.

"General Jackson," he said quietly, "I am Bill Weatherford."

Jackson was amazed. "Mr. Weatherford," he said, "after what you did at Fort Mims—how *dare* you!"

"I am alone," replied the man the Creeks knew as Red Eagle. "Do with me as you like. I am in your power. I have done the white people all the harm I could. And if I had any warriors left I would fight to the last. But please, spare the women and the children."

When Jackson's men found out Red Eagle was in their camp, they wanted to hang him. But Jackson was impressed by the man's quiet courage. "I ordered you brought to me in chains," Jackson told him. "But you have come of your own free will. You are not in my power. Return to your people, and fight if you can."

"With what shall I fight?" asked the Indian. "With dead warriors? You have destroyed us."

Chapter 8

"LIKE WILD HORSES"

The air in the council house was thick with the smoke of the peace pipe. Bill McIntosh, chief of the Lower Creeks, smiled as he passed it to the Indian agents sitting across from him. They understood each other very well.

The agents had offered McIntosh thousands of dollars if he would sign the piece of paper they had brought. Thousands of dollars would also be given to any other chiefs he could convince to sign. They would give this money to McIntosh and the chiefs in secret, however. For the money was a bribe.

The paper the agents wanted the chiefs to sign was a sale agreement. The eastern Creek lands in the state of Georgia would go to the United States. In exchange, the United States would give the Creeks new land on the Arkansas River. This land was far to the west, beyond the Mississippi River, in what is now Oklahoma.

McIntosh smiled to the agents, but he looked at

the agreement with a heavy heart. He loved the land of his Indian ancestors as much as any Creek. But he was half white, and he understood the white man's ways. There would be more and more settlers as the years passed. The Creeks would never be safe. Perhaps, beyond the great river . . . He picked up the quill pen.

Suddenly, one of the other Indians in the council house stood up. It was the young chief, Opothle Yahola, a friend of Menewa. He walked over and stood directly in front of McIntosh. He pointed down at the paper.

"You know the law!" he said fiercely.

For a moment McIntosh's eyes met those of Opothle Yahola. The Creeks are a stubborn people, McIntosh thought. Some of them will never learn. It was true, the Creeks had passed a law forbidding the sale of Creek lands, except by the entire Creek nation. If he signed this agreement, he would be breaking the law. McIntosh knew the law well, for it was he who first suggested it to the Creek council. But now what did Creek law mean to the Whites?

The Congress of the United States recognized that the sale of land by McIntosh was not right. But it still forced it on the Creeks.

After the Red Stick War, General Jackson had taken away more than half of the Creeks' lands—a wide strip along the border with Florida, and a great chunk of rich land in Alabama. Jackson had promised them then that their remaining lands would be safe. But Jackson lied, and McIntosh knew it. Jackson, and men like him, would never stop until all the Indians were moved beyond the Mississippi. Better to accept it peacefully than wait until it was forced on them with more bloodshed.

Opothle Yahola turns his back on McIntosh signing away Creek lands.

McIntosh signed the agreement. Opothle Yahola watched him with burning eyes. Then he turned on his heel and walked out. Other chiefs got up and followed. Of those that remained, some signed, others waved the paper away, shaking their heads. For they knew the Creek law. Punishment for signing away Creek lands without permission of the tribal council was death.

Opothle Yahola rode swiftly to the village of Menewa, now the leader of the Upper Creeks. When Menewa heard his story, he called a council of all the Upper Creeks. He then told the council what McIntosh had done. The council heard the evidence and passed judgment. Those who signed the agreement must die.

Menewa himself led the band of warriors to the home of Bill McIntosh and surrounded it. McIntosh had visitors, including white men. Menewa ordered women, children, and the white men out of the building. Then he set fire to the house. When McIntosh and another Creek who had signed the agreement ran out, the Creeks shot them down.

William McIntosh

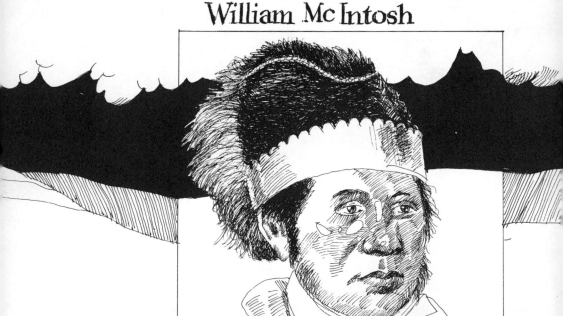

Menewa hoped that in this way he would show the Americans that the Creeks would hold onto their lands at all costs. Jackson had paid them nothing for the land. He had only promised them no one would take away any more lands. But since then, more Georgia settlers had been moving onto Creek lands. And now Alabama settlers were doing the same. And, to the south were the Florida settlers, now American since Spain sold its territory to the United States. So the Creek lands were surrounded.

In 1828, Andrew Jackson was elected President of the United States. His policy toward the Creeks was the same as the preceding presidents' except that Jackson was ready to use force to make the Indians move. He

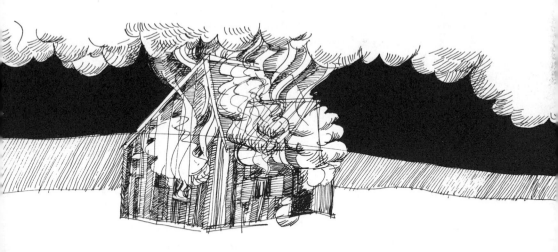

quickly informed the Creeks, Choctaws, Cherokees, Chickasaws and Seminoles that they would all have to move west of the Mississippi. For Jackson believed Indians had no rights. Either they moved out of the way of the white settlers, or they would be destroyed.

The same year Jackson was elected president, the first Creeks arrived in the lands to the west. They soon sent word back to their brothers in the east that the winters were bitterly cold, but the land was good.

Meanwhile, in Alabama, the Creeks' situation grew rapidly worse. President Jackson made it clear to the white citizens of Alabama that they had nothing to fear from the federal government, no matter what they did to the Creeks. So the Alabamans were soon doing a great deal: burning Creek houses, shooting unarmed Creek men and women, trampling crops of corn and beans, stealing or killing cattle and hogs. Under the new state law, no Creek could appear in court as a witness against a white man. So the settlers were never punished for their crimes. But if a Creek tried to defend himself against attack, he was punished.

At last, the Creeks gave up. They notified Jackson that they were ready now to sell all their land and move to the west.

Many Creeks, however, did not want to move from the lands of their ancestors. So it was agreed, when the land was sold, that any Creek family that wanted to could stay behind. Each family would be given a small farm of its own, to work in the white man's way. Or they could sell the farm if they chose.

Unfortunately, the white settlers of Alabama ignored the terms of the treaty entirely. Once they knew the land was to be sold, the settlers swarmed onto it without even waiting for the Creeks to pack up for the long journey west. The Creeks were driven off their land or shot if they tried to remain. And those who were not driven off were soon cheated. It was easy to claim that a Creek had sold his land—the Creek could not appear in court to say no!

Within a few months, thousands of Creeks roamed the countryside, without shelter, blankets, adequate clothing, or food. They appeared at the edge of the towns to beg for food. Others, unable to live by begging, stole. This led the white settlers to claim the Creeks had gone on the warpath again and demand protection. And Jackson promptly sent troops.

Jackson abandoned the terms of the treaty. All Creeks must leave Alabama, he said. Right away. None could remain. Some of the Indians who had been raiding white settlements were rounded up by United States government troops. Put in chains, they were marched without food for ninety miles to Montgomery. From Montgomery, they were put on boats and shipped to the west, but not before one old man cut his throat in protest.

Thousands of Creeks moved westward. Some had to walk the whole distance—almost a thousand miles. Others took turns riding horses, or riding in wagons. Those who weakened were left to die as the troops forced the marchers to keep moving. Many starved, or died of the cold.

Thousands were crowded onto steamships, which terrified them. Worse still, many caught cholera and dysentery and died. And when the steamboat *Monmouth* sank, 300 Creeks drowned.

Others died before they ever left Alabama, victims of starvation, or of the Alabama settlers. Still others ran

away to join their brothers, the Seminoles, in Florida. A few tried to join the Cherokees in northern Georgia, but were turned back or shot by the Georgians.

And even when the Creeks reached their new lands, their suffering didn't end. It was a raw land. Corn and pumpkins and beans had to be planted— they did not grow wild. The food and blankets, the guns for hunting, the pots and pans and horses, promised by the United States—where were they? The Creeks had somehow to make a living from this wilderness with their bare hands, and what little they had been able to bring with them as they were hurried out of Alabama.

One old Creek complained of their treatment:

"Our road has been a hard one, and on it we have left the bones of our great men, our women and children. We wanted to harvest our crops, and we wanted to go in peace and friendship. Did we? No! We were driven off like wolves! Our people's feet were bleeding. We are men. We have women and children. Why then should we come like wild horses?"

Chapter 9

PIONEERS

Never again would the sacred Creek council fires struggle with the night shadows along the rivers of Alabama. Never again would the shrill cry of the Green Corn Dance be heard in Georgia. A whole nation had been torn from its ancient homeland. And now it faced a difficult and unfamiliar wilderness.

The Creeks settled along the Arkansas, Verdigris and Canadian Rivers, in northeastern Oklahoma Territory, not far from the present city of Tulsa. They stayed in the eastern part of the land given them. One reason for this was that they wanted to be near Fort Gibson, at the fork of the Arkansas and Verdigris Rivers. At Fort Gibson, they could get supplies. But another reason was that it was in the east that their new land most resembled the old. In the east, along the rivers, there were forests. To the west was prairie—flat land covered by thick high grass. To the Creeks, the prairie seemed useless.

The prairie was also dangerous. For there, the fierce

Osage and Pawnee Indians hunted. These Indians were very different from the Creek. They did not farm, but lived by hunting. Their young men seemed to live on the backs of their horses, and they were much more skillful riders than the Creeks. Years of war with the Cherokees and other Indians in the Arkansas Territory had weakened the Osage, but they were still a fierce and proud people.

At first, the Creeks built their villages right beside the rivers and streams, just as they had in Alabama and Georgia. But they soon learned that this was a mistake. For in this new land, a rainstorm meant a sudden flood. The rivers would rise quickly and sweep away the Creek villages they had worked so hard to build. Still, they built the villages as close to the streams as was safe.

The weather was nothing like the weather in their old lands. The summers were long, hot, and dry. The winters were bitterly cold, and snow was common. And the Creeks had hardly ever seen snow. Perhaps worst of all, sudden storms seemed to strike out of nowhere, blowing their log houses about like leaves.

The first years were by far the hardest. When the Creeks gave up their old lands, the United States had promised them supplies to help them over the first year or two—flour, cornmeal, meat, pots and pans, guns for hunting. But the supplies did not come in time. And when they did come, the meat was rotten, the flour was full of insects. Certain traders were cheating the Creeks—and the government, who paid for the supplies.

But, like other pioneers, the Creeks found a way to survive. They had no guns so they relearned the art of the bow and arrow. Then they ventured onto the prairies to hunt the great buffalo who roamed there in countless numbers. They learned to make pots and pans out of dried clay. They made stoves out of dried mud (adobe) to keep them warm through the terrible winter.

Like other pioneers, they had to defend themselves against Indians. The Osage, Pawnees, and Kiowas sometimes raided their villages, mostly to steal horses. The Creeks did not ride as well as the Osage, but they still knew how to fight. They taught the Indians of the Great Plains to respect them and soon made friends with them.

The Creeks had other neighbors. Many Cherokees had moved west from the Arkansas Territory even before the Creeks arrived. They were joined by more Cherokees who had been forced to leave their lands in Georgia and Tennessee. And then the Choctaws, Chickasaws, and even some of the Florida Seminoles were forced to move west as well. All of these Indians, like the Creeks, built villages and farmed. And so these five tribes, because they were so different from the warlike Great Plains Indians, were called "the Five Civilized Tribes."

The Creeks adopted a written constitution and code of laws similar to that of the United States. They called themselves the Creek Republic. Their tribal council now was made up of delegates elected from each of the villages. And each village had its own town council of elected delegates as well. Courts were established and judges elected. Some Creeks became "light horsemen." These were policemen who rode about the country on horseback, enforcing the Creek laws.

The years passed, and the Creeks gradually got used to the new land. Most still farmed together, in the old way, clearing, planting, and harvesting the land of the whole village. But some Creeks managed to bring their wealth from the east. These, who were mostly mixed-bloods, owned large farms and had black and Indian slaves to work for them. While the poorer Creeks wanted to live much as their ancestors had, the wealthier ones wanted to adopt the white man's ways as much as possible. And so the two sides often quarrelled.

From their villages, the Creeks watched the United States grow rapidly around them. They saw settlers travel west across the Creek lands to faraway California. Others were traveling south to Texas, which was Mexican territory at that time. Then the Texans rebelled, led by Sam Houston, the Creeks' enemy in the Red Stick war. When the United States accepted Texas as a new state, Mexico declared war. The United States quickly won, and took from Mexico all the land from Texas to California. The Creeks had once been on the western frontier of the United States. Now the United States reached from ocean to ocean. And settlers flooded around and past the Creeks on all sides.

A typical Creek house of the period.

Not all the white settlers who traveled through the Creek country continued on their way. Some settled on Creek land. This was against Creek law. But again Creek law proved difficult to enforce. The light horsemen removed the white settlers, but the settlers soon came back. Besides, some Creeks encouraged the white settlers by renting land to them.

The United States suggested that the Indian Territory become a state. The Creeks and Cherokees called a council of all the Indians to consider the idea. If the Indian Territory became a state, the separate Indian republics would have to be broken up. The villages would no longer own the land together, or in common, but each family would have its own farm. White settlers could move in and buy land. The Creeks, remembering what had happened to those who had tried to farm this way in Alabama, urged the other Indians to reject statehood. And they did. Almost in one voice, the Indian republics said no to becoming a state.

And so the Creeks might have continued, living in the old way, slowly adapting to the white man's way. But once again a war, the War Between the States (Civil War) changed everything. And once again the Creeks were unable to stay out. And, just as the Civil War divided the United States, it divided the Creek Republic, and sent Creek to fight against Creek.

Chapter 10

"AND NOW THE WOLF HAS COME"

The Civil War began when the southern states tried to secede, or separate themselves from the United States. The southern states wanted to secede because they thought the federal government intended to end slavery. The great plantations of the South depended upon the cheap labor of slaves for their profits.

Abraham Lincoln refused to allow the South to secede. The southern states rebelled and formed themselves into the Confederate States of America, which is usually called the "Confederacy." The states that remained loyal to Lincoln were still, officially, the United States of America, but usually they were known as the "Union" or "North" during the Civil War.

The Five Civilized Tribes came from the South. Many among them had owned slaves at one time or another. The South expected the Five Tribes to join in the war on their side. The Confederacy sent agents to talk to the Indians. The agents guaranteed that the Confederate States would honor all the treaties made between the tribes and the Confederacy.

Again the Creeks were divided. Some, especially the wealthier mixed-bloods, sided with the South. When the Creek council held a meeting to decide what to do, these wealthier Creeks took control. Those who opposed them left the meeting. The result was that the council voted to join the South.

In the meantime, troops of the Confederacy marched into Indian Territory from Texas, one of the Confederate states. Union troops within the Indian Territory were gradually pulled out, because they were needed more urgently farther north in Kansas, and in the East where the main battles of the Civil War were being fought. So during the early part of the Civil War, Confederate troops, including their Indian regiments, were able to conquer most of the Indian Territory.

Despite the fact that many Creeks fought with the South, many others believed that their nation should remain loyal to the United States. Led by Opothle Yahola, now an old man, they refused to join the Confederacy. These loyal Creeks killed their cattle, dried the meat, and set out on a long march north into Kansas. More than half the tribe followed Yahola on this march. They went to Kansas because that was the nearest area that had been freed of Confederate control at the time. On the way there, they were attacked by the Texans and also by the Confederate Creeks, but they successfully drove off the attackers.

When they reached Kansas, the loyal Creeks tried to find the Indian agent of the United States to declare their loyalty. But the United States no longer had any Indian agents in the area. Their former agents had joined the Confederacy.

The band of loyal Creeks had no place to live. So they had to camp out in the open through the bitter winter.

Eventually, they found an agent. But by that time, the United States had declared the entire Creek nation rebels. All treaties were canceled. And in Kansas, the nearly 8,000 men, women and children with Opothle Yahola were dying of starvation and the cold. So Opothle Yahola wrote to President Lincoln.

The United States promised to protect the Creeks from all enemies, Indian or white, he wrote. "But now the wolf is come. Men who are strangers tread our soil. When we made our treaty in Washington the President assured us that our children would laugh around our houses without fear, and we believed it. I was at Washington when the treaty was signed. Now white people are trying to take our people away to fight against us and against you. I am alive. I well remember the treaty. My ears are open and my memory is good."

But in Washington, the ears were not open and the memory was not good. The Creeks were forgotten. They were left to defend themselves and their land as best they could.

The loyal Creeks formed a regiment of soldiers. With white officers commanding them, this regiment

General Ulysses S. Grant, victor.

marched back into the Indian Territory, in 1863. There it met Creeks fighting for the Confederacy in a series of small battles. The Confederate Creeks were driven out and the Union Creeks took over Fort Gibson. But then the white officers, who also had little to eat, rebelled against their commanding officer and fled to Kansas. The Creeks remained.

Months later, more United States troops arrived to help keep the Indian Territory clear of the Confederates. At the battles of Honey Springs and Cabin Creek, in July of 1863, the Confederate Creeks and Texans were defeated. These places are near the present city of Tulsa, in northeast Oklahoma.

The war finally ended in 1865. The North had won, but the cost in lives was high. Now the two sides would have to learn to live side by side in peace again.

General Robert E. Lee, vanquished.

The Creeks slowly drifted back into the Indian Territory. They, too, had lost many lives—in the battles, and through cold and starvation. They, too, would have to forget the war that had divided them, to rebuild their towns and farms together once again.

But even as the Creeks tried to settle in and rebuild their lives, they received terrible news. The United States had decided to take away more than half their lands! They were being punished for joining the Confederacy, even though as many Creeks had fought for the North as had fought for the South.

Many of the Creeks were still alive who had signed the 1832 treaty with President Andrew Jackson. They remembered the promises in that treaty. The land in the west was to be theirs "as long as the rivers run." So how could the United States take it away?

They were told that the Congress had simply torn up the old treaties. Now they must sign a new treaty, and in this treaty the whole western half of their lands must be given up. These western lands would in turn be given to Pawnees, Arapahoes, and Cheyennes. Some of the land would also be given to the former slaves of the Creeks.

Once again, as so many times before, the Creeks really had no choice. So they signed this treaty of 1866. And they set about helping their new neighbors learn to farm the land that was once theirs. The Creeks also contacted some of the Indians even farther west, like the Comanches, Apaches, and Sioux. These Indians were still fighting the Whites. The Creeks tried to convince them to live in peace. When the Sioux killed General George Custer and his troops at the Battle of Little Big Horn in 1876, the Creeks invited the Sioux to come and share the Creek lands and live in peace.

For they had no fear of any Indians.

In fact, the Creeks began to see that the more Indians who settled in the Indian Territory, the better. Already white settlers were moving in to some of the unoccupied western lands in the Creeks' section of Indian Territory. The Creeks hoped that all the Indians might come together and so hold on to the land.

Much of the western territory was tall-grass prairies (flat, grassy plains). A few Creeks became ranchers. But most of their land remained unused. Then, in the 1870s, white people discovered that these tall-grass prairies were the very best range lands for

The booming cattle business made the tall-grass prairies desirable to white ranchers.

cattle. And cattle were in great demand for meat to feed the hungry populations of the cities. So before long, white men demanded a chance to buy this land from the Indians. This grass was as high as a man on horseback and wild—it would cost nothing to graze cattle on it. Cattle could be fed on it year-round—the grass did not die in winter. The cattle could be sold at a large profit. In fact, a railroad reached Fort Gibson in 1871, and by 1872 had been built clear through the Creek Republic. Its main purpose was to carry cattle north to the markets at Kansas City, and St. Louis.

Congress considered the prairie lands much too valuable to leave with the Creeks. They thought the Creeks were wasting it, since they were not using it.

The members of Congress were also convinced that the Creek way of life was bad for them. Owning land in common, working just enough to get by—that was not the white man's way. The Whites believed that the work of each person was what counted. The more a person worked, the more he earned. But the Creeks owned everything together, and so no man could lift himself above the others. Because of this way of life, the Creeks did not work their land as much as they could have.

So Congress decided to break up the Creek Republic, as well as the other republics of the Five Civilized Tribes. Each Creek family was to be given a farm, and the land that was left over would be sold to white settlers, with the money divided among the Creeks.

The Creeks did not want to give up their republic or break up their lands. But Congress ignored the wishes of the Indians, just as it had ignored all the treaties with the Creek nation.

82

Chapter 11

THE END OF THE CREEK NATION

The Congress of the United States found itself in a dilemma. When the Congress tried to give Creek families their farms, they found that too many people were claiming to be Creeks. And too few Creeks were claiming their farms.

Men and women had come from all over the United States claiming to be Creeks. An investigation found that most of these people were not Creeks at all, but were trying to get the free land. On the other hand, there were countless Creeks actually living on their lands who refused to come to Fort Gibson and take legal possession of the farms that were to be given to them.

Congress appointed a special committee to look into the matter. The committee called in some of the Creeks who refused to take their farms and asked them why. And again and again the Congressmen heard the same answer.

One by one, the Creeks told them that they still held to the treaty with President Jackson, the treaty of 1832. That treaty gave the Creek people the land forever, and President Jackson himself had signed it.

The Congressmen impatiently explained: that treaty was no longer in effect, it had been changed. The Creeks would have to take individual farms now. The Creek nation was no more. The Indian Territory was being joined to the Oklahoma Territory to become a new state, Oklahoma.

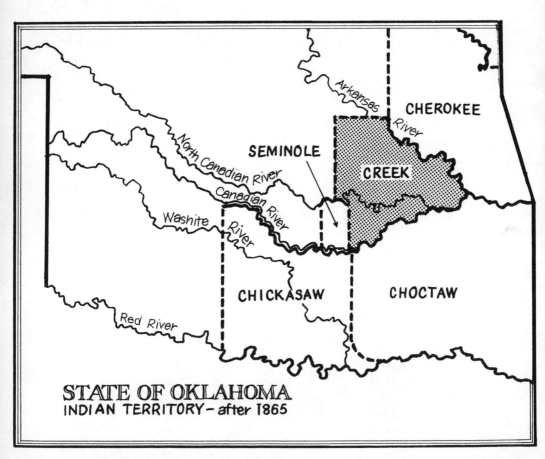

STATE OF OKLAHOMA
INDIAN TERRITORY – after 1865

But this "Oklahoma Territory"—what was that? asked the Indians. Wasn't that their land, promised to them in the treaty of 1832? And hadn't they been forced to give that land to the other Indians—the Pawnees, and the Cheyennes, and the others? Like the other Civilized Tribes they had given up that land so those tribes of the plains would have a place to live.

And what had happened to those plains Indians? The Creeks and the other Civilized Tribes had taught them how to farm, how to work together planting and harvesting. And then the white men had come and forced them to take small farms—as they were doing to the Creeks now. And before long, all the land belonged to white men and there were hardly any Indian lands left, though they called it "Oklahoma"—Land of the Red Man.

No, the Creeks said. They did not want that. They wanted their own lands as always, to belong to the whole tribe. And they had President Jackson's promise.

One old Creek, named Crazy Snake, waved a piece of paper at the committee. It was a copy of the Treaty of 1832. He wanted to call the other tribes to witness what it said and what it meant.

The chairman of the committee was impatient. Did he mean the other Civilized Tribes?

No, replied Crazy Snake. "I do not mean the other four Civilized Tribes, but I can call on the Spanish government and the British government and the French government—I can call on the civilized governments across the Mother of Waters to come in and see that this is right."

The year was 1906. Crazy Snake did not know that the European countries had long ago lost interest in how the United States dealt with the Indians. He was not an educated man. But he knew history, because he had lived it. He knew the white man had promised him this land forever, and he reminded the committee:

"He (Jackson) said as long as the sun shines and the sky is up yonder this agreement will be kept. As long as the light is with us it shall last. As long as the grass grows it shall last. As long as the waters run it shall last. That is what he said and we believed it. The grass is growing, the waters run, the sun shines, the light is with us, and the agreement is with us yet. For the God that is above us all witnessed that agreement."

Crazy Snake did not convince the committee to change its mind, of course. But Crazy Snake's mind was not easily changed either. He led some of his people far up into the hills of what was once their land. There they tried to live as always, to farm the land together as always. But troops chased them down and brought them to prison. They were not released until they agreed to accept the farms set aside for them.

The white man's way did not work out for the Creeks much better than it had for the plains Indians. Congress, fearing that the full-blooded Creeks would be cheated of their land, ordered that their land could not be sold. But the land of the mixed-bloods could be sold. And Oklahoma was soon swarming with whites trying to cheat the mixed-bloods of their land. And many of these Creeks were cheated. Within a few years, most of the Creeks' land was in the hands of white men.

Then oil was discovered—right under the little farms forced upon the followers of Crazy Snake! Overnight, these Indians were rich. Some of them were actually millionaires. Had the oil been discovered before the Creek Republic was broken up, the oil would have belonged to the whole tribe. Now it belonged to a few Indians, and to white men who had managed to buy some of the Indian lands.

Some of the Creeks who now found themselves rich had never wanted anything more than to live as their ancestors lived. They did not know what to do with the thousands of dollars that began to fill their bank accounts. When they spent this money foolishly, people laughed at them.

And as a few Creeks became very rich, many more grew poorer and poorer. Many lost their lands. Others found the land they had was not enough to provide for their families. More and more Creeks left the land for the new cities and towns of Oklahoma. The Creek nation had been destroyed.

Crazy Snake

Chapter 12

THE CREEKS TODAY

The Creek Republic, the Creek nation, the Creek tribe—all disappeared. But not the Creek people.

Creeks have become important and valuable citizens of their state, Oklahoma, and of their nation, the United States. Some have earned positions of political leadship. They have become doctors, lawyers, engineers, soldiers, mechanics and teachers, pipefitters and surveyors, factory workers and farmers.

But the years since statehood have not been easy for many Creeks. Hundreds of Creeks held stubbornly to their farms, though many men tried to take them away. These Creeks remained in the small villages far from the state's new highways. Although they could no longer own land in common, they could still help each other, and they did. And so they survived even the hardest times. They still took the Black Drink and danced the Green Corn Dance at mid-summer. They played stickball as fiercely as their ancestors, and threw

A Creek surveyor marks today's boundary lines.

their spears in the chunkey yards. They loved the old ways and would not give them up.

The Indian Bureau thought that these Creeks would always be poor if they remained in their villages. In the cities, they could begin a new life. So, in 1950, the United States tried a new policy on these poorest Creeks. They moved them away from their villages. In fact, they moved them out of the whole state of Oklahoma. The Indians were taken to large cities, the largest number to Los Angeles.

For a few years, some Creeks tried this plan. But before long, they began drifting back to their old villages. The plan did not work. Even for the very poorest Creeks, the familiar village, with friends, relatives, chunkey yard and the old traditions, was better than the crowded cities of the white men.

Today, many of these Creeks still live in their villages. But the state of Oklahoma and the government of the United States now help them where they are. They are no longer as poor as they once were. And they still have pride in what they are—Creeks. They know that their history, so full of suffering and courage, has become a part of the history of the United States, a history all Americans share.

The gift of the Creek people to our history was summed up by one of the greatest Creek chiefs, named Pleasant Porter:

"The vitality of our race still persists," he said. "We have not lived for nothing. We are the original discoverers of this continent and the conquerors of it from the animal kingdom. The European nations found us here and learned that it was possible for men to exist here. We have given our thought forces. The best blood of our ancestors has mixed with that of the white statesmen and leading citizens. We have made ourselves an indestructible element of their national history. The race that has rendered this service to the other nations of mankind cannot utterly perish."

INDEX

F
Five Civilized Tribes, 72, 75, 76, 82
Flint River, 13, 24
Florida, 23, 26, 29, 32, 34, 38, 40, 62, 65, 69, 72
Fort Gibson, 70, 79, 82, 83
Fort Mims, 53, 54, 59
Fort Toulouse, 34
France, 26, 27-28, 29, 33, 34, 36, 38, 85
French and Indian War, 36

G
George II, 30, 33, 34
Georgia, 13, 22, 24, 30-34, 38, 39, 40, 41, 42, 43, 46, 51, 52, 61, 65, 69, 70, 71, 72
Great Britain, 26, 28, 30-33, 34, 36, 37-40, 44, 45, 46, 48, 49, 51, 52, 85
Green Corn Dance, 20-21, 70, 88

H
Hawkins, Benjamin, 44-48
Honey Springs, Battle of, 79
Houston, Sam, 58, 73

I
Ichisi, 23-24
Indian Bureau, 90

J
Jackson, Andrew, 54-60, 62, 65, 66, 67, 80, 84, 85, 86

K
Kansas, 76, 77
Kansas City, 82
Kiowas, 72
Knox, Henry, 42, 46

L
Little Big Horn, Battle of, 80
Lincoln, Abraham, 75, 77
London, 30, 33, 42
Los Angeles, 90

Louisiana, 36, 41, 49

M
Madison, James, 59
Maryland, 43
Massachusetts, 28
Master of Breath (Great Spirit), 9, 10, 11, 20, 41
McGillivray, Alexander, 39-40, 41, 42, 43
McIntosh, William, 51, 52, 58, 61-64
Menewa, 51, 52, 55, 58-59, 64
Mexico, 13, 27, 73
mico, 13, 24, 25, 26, 37, 41, 45
Mississippi River, 27, 40, 49, 61, 62, 66
Mobile, 28, 29, 39
Monmouth (steamboat), 68
Montgomery, Alabama, 67
Muscogee, 9, 10, 11, 12, 13

N
New Orleans, 28, 59
New York City, 42, 43
North Carolina, 24, 43

O
Oglethorpe, James, 30, 32-33
Ohio River, 48, 49
Oklahoma (Indian Territory), 61, 70, 74, 76, 79, 80, 81, 84, 85, 86, 87, 88, 90
Opothle Yahola, 62, 63, 64, 76, 77
Osage, 71, 72

P
Pawnees, 71, 72, 80
Pennsylvania, 43
Pensacola, 38, 39, 41, 51
Porter, Pleasant, 90-91
prairie, 70, 71, 81
"The Prophet," 47

R
railroads, 82
Red Stick Creeks, 51, 52, 53, 55-59
Red Stick War, 51-60, 62, 73